Alien Adventures

The Sands of Akwa

Elen Caldecott ● Jonatronix

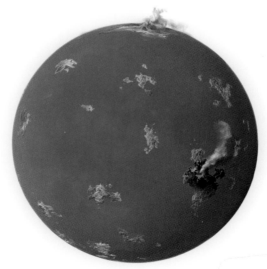

T0346912

OXFORD
UNIVERSITY PRESS

Max's mission log

We are travelling through space on board the micro-ship Excelsa with our new friends, Nok and Seven.

We're on a mission to save Planet Exis (Nok's home planet), which is running out of power. We need to collect four fragments that have been hidden throughout the Beta-Prime Galaxy. Together the fragments form the Core of Exis. Only the Core will restore power to the planet.

It's not easy. A space villain called Badlaw wants the power of the Core for himself. His army of robotic Krools is never far behind us!

Fragments collected so far: 0

In our last adventure ...

Ant and Tiger were trying to fix the fabricator (a machine that can copy and make anything). The fabricator went wrong and we ended up with four Tigers!

Then we were chased by Badlaw's Krools. We managed to trick them and get away!

We have just reached Planet Akwa where we hope to find the first fragment.

Planet Akwa

Planet Akwa is a large planet mostly covered by water. There are islands that poke up out of the ocean. These have sandy beaches with large black rocks on them.

Known life forms

- Akwans
- Raptiss

Surface conditions

- Mostly water
- Warm temperatures
- Volcanic islands

islands

ocean

yellow sky

volcanic island

The micro-ship landed gently on the sandy shore.

"Planet Akwa," Ant said, as he stepped off the ship. He breathed in the warm, salty air.

"Where shall we start looking for the fragment?" asked Tiger.

Nok looked along the beach. "Let's try this way," he said.

"It will be easier if we are normal size," said Max.

They pressed their buttons and grew. Then they set off down the beach.

They had not gone far when Cat came
to a sudden stop.

"I thought I heard something," she said.
"It sounded like whispering."

They looked around but the beach
was empty.

"I'm sure it was nothing," Max said.

They were about to set off again when Tiger spotted a shadow moving behind the rocks. "Over there!" he said, pointing.

Seven scanned the rocks. "I'm picking up traces of life forms," he said.

"Is anyone there?" Max called.

Silently, four strange creatures stepped out from behind the rocks. They were tall, with spotted skin and eyes the colour of the sea.

One of the creatures stepped forwards.

"I am Livi, an Akwan warrior. Who are you and what are you doing here?" she snapped.

"I'm Nok, from Exis ..."

Before Nok could finish, an ear-splitting scream came from above.

"What was that?" Ant cried.

"Raptiss!" one of the Akwans yelled.

Just then a huge shadow was cast over the beach.

The Akwans dived into the sea. Only Livi was left on the beach.

"Get out of the open! Quickly!" she shouted.

Another scream split the sky. The friends looked up and saw a massive creature with sharp claws and teeth. It was a Raptiss. More Raptiss were circling in the sky above.

Their jaws snapped like giant scissors.
Their screeches sounded like metal
scraping against metal.

Then one dived towards the beach.

The friends scattered.

Cat and Tiger sprinted down the beach.
Seven was right behind them.

"Shrink!" Cat yelled.

They pressed their buttons and shrank.
Then they hurried to the shelter of
the cliffs.

At the same time, Max, Ant, Nok and Livi were sprinting the other way. The cries of the Raptiss pierced the air above them.

Then one Raptiss twisted in the sky. It hurtled towards Livi.

"No!" cried Ant.

Ant pulled Livi to one side. The sharp beak of the Raptiss just missed her.

The Raptiss circled. Then it screamed and dived towards Livi again, its claws outstretched.

"We have to stop it!" Nok shouted.
"Follow me!"

He pressed the button on his suit to
activate his wings. Max and Ant did
the same.

The three friends shot into the sky, straight at the Raptiss. They buzzed around it like flies. The Raptiss twitched and jerked away, taking its eyes off Livi.

The Raptiss did not look where it was flying. It slammed into another Raptiss. The two screamed at each other.

As the Raptiss started to fight, Max, Ant and Nok flew back down to Livi.

"You can fly like the Raptiss!" said a startled Livi.

"We can do lots more than that!" said Ant.

"Let's get into the water while the Raptiss are fighting," said Max.

Max used his watch to call Seven. "Are you safe?"

"Yes," Seven replied. "We are OK."

"We'll have to stay split up for now," Max said. "You search the islands for the fragment. We'll search underwater."

"Be careful," Seven replied.

"You saved me," Livi said. "You are warriors, too!"

"We're on a mission. Maybe you can help?" Nok asked.

"I will take you to our leader," Livi said. "Come, follow me."

Find out what happens next in *Holo-board Havoc.*